Building Jewish Identity
VOLUMES 1-2

Teacher's Lesson Plan Manual
By Sharon Halper

Project Editors: Aviva Werner, Dena Neusner
Design: AURAS Design
Copyright © 2012 Behrman House, Inc.
Springfield, New Jersey
ISBN 978-0-87441-862-0 • Printed in the U.S.A.

www.behrmanhouse.com
www.behrmanhouse.com/building-jewish-identity

CONTENTS

Introduction
- Structure of the Textbooks 3
- Structure of This Lesson Plan Manual 3
- Using This Lesson Plan Manual 4
- Experiential Learning 4
- Using Technology 4
- Teaching Strategies 5
- Being Inclusive 6

Part 1: Lesson Plans for Volume 1: Our Community
- Chapter 1: Jewish Like Me 8
- Chapter 2: Pieces of the Puzzle: Jewish Community 10
- Chapter 3: A Rich Heritage: History and Stories 12
- Chapter 4: Speaking the Same Language: Hebrew 14
- Chapter 5: Learning by Doing: Symbols and Rituals 16
- Chapter 6: Becoming Our Best Selves: Mitzvot 18
- Chapter 7: Your Jewish Identity 20

Part 2: Lesson Plans for Volume 2: Sacred Time
- Chapter 1: Times of Your Life 22
- Chapter 2: Making Time for the Jewish Week 24
- Chapter 3: Celebrating the Jewish Year 26
- Chapter 4: The First Steps in a Jewish Life 28
- Chapter 5: Preparing to Be a Jewish Adult 30
- Chapter 6: Establishing a Jewish Home 32
- Chapter 7: Mourning a Loss the Jewish Way 34
- Chapter 8: This Jewish Life 36

Part 3: Activities for Jewish Holidays
- Introduction 38
- Activity 1: High Holidays (Rosh Hashanah and Yom Kippur) 39
- Activity 2: Sukkot 39
- Activity 3: Simḥat Torah 40
- Activity 4: Ḥanukkah 40
- Activity 5: Tu BiShevat 41
- Activity 6: Purim 42
- Activity 7: Passover 42
- Activity 8: Yom Ha'atzma'ut 43
- Activity 9: Shavuot 43

Part 4: Family Education Programs
- Introduction 44
- Keep in Mind 44
- Techniques to Use with Families 45

Assessments 47

INTRODUCTION

STRUCTURE OF THE TEXTBOOKS

The *Building Jewish Identity* series introduces students to core knowledge that is essential to developing a strong Jewish identity. Each volume uses stories, interviews, and activities to explore the myths, laws, language, symbols, rituals, and ethical teachings that create a distinctive Jewish worldview.

Volume 1: Our Community introduces students to the idea of Jewish community and helps them discover how our community brings us together, connecting us with our Jewish identity.

Volume 2: Sacred Time: The Jewish Calendar and Life Cycle introduces the Jewish concept of time and explores how the Jewish calendar and life cycle help us celebrate important moments, providing a lifelong connection to our heritage, culture, and values.

Both volumes include these features:

- **Your Turn:** Experiential activities, such as designing a Jewish ritual object
- **Meet … :** Interviews with real kids, about how their Jewish identity helps define their lives
- **Talk about It:** Review questions for reflection and discussion
- **Words to Know:** Important concepts introduced in the text

STRUCTURE OF THIS LESSON PLAN MANUAL

Part 1 of this Lesson Plan Manual presents 13 ready-to-use lesson plans of approximately 50 minutes each for *Building Jewish Identity Volume 1: Our Community*.

Part 2 presents 16 ready-to-use lesson plans of approximately 50 minutes each for *Building Jewish Identity Volume 2: Sacred Time: The Jewish Calendar and Life Cycle*.

Each lesson plan includes:

- **Essential Question:** A primary question that reflects the main idea of the lesson
- **Lesson Objectives:** Goals that students will achieve by the end of the lesson
- **Getting Started:** Ways to energize your students for the lesson and activities to come
- **Exploring the Text:** A step-by-step guide for presenting the lesson with a variety of activities, including numerous experiential learning activities
- **Wrapping It Up:** A brief activity to review and tie the main themes of the lesson together
- **The Tech Connection:** Ideas for engaging your students in further learning activities using technology, as well as multimedia resources and methodologies to supplement learning

Part 3 of this Lesson Plan Manual presents activities for teaching the Jewish holidays through the lens of building Jewish identity and many of the concepts introduced in the textbooks.

Part 4 provides ideas for creating Family Education Programs for Jewish learning and identity development involving students and families together.

The **Assessments** section at the end of this manual provides opportunities for students to demonstrate their understanding, in order to help you determine the effectiveness of each lesson and the individual needs of each student.

USING THIS LESSON PLAN MANUAL

At the start of the school year, map out when you plan to teach each chapter. The 29 lessons in Parts 1 and 2 of this manual have been designed so you can teach an average of one lesson per week from the textbooks. In addition, you can use activities in the Jewish Holidays section of this manual at appropriate times of the year to help students make personal meaning through the building blocks of Jewish identity that are woven into our holiday observances.

Before you begin to teach a chapter from either of the *Building Jewish Identity* textbooks, read through this Lesson Plan Manual to familiarize yourself with the chapter. You may choose to use the lessons as written or adapt them to fit the needs of your class. If you decide to adapt, be sure to frame your lesson around an essential question, either the one suggested or one of your own that points to the main idea of the lesson.

Plan to use the Family Education ideas in this manual throughout the year, to engage parents as your partners in developing students' Jewish identity.

EXPERIENTIAL LEARNING

Each lesson plan includes suggestions for experiential learning. Learning can be accomplished through reading, seeing, and hearing about the experiences of others. But the *most successful* learning occurs when we experience something ourselves.

- The experiential learning component of these lessons asks students to take the content of the lesson and dynamically transform it through a process of reflection, problem solving, and analysis.
- Experiential learning helps students learn about themselves. Much like trying a new food, students discover their tastes and explore new ones as they try on new responses and grow their understanding and abilities.
- Experiential learning models the partnership of formal and informal learning, valuing both as parts of our Jewish identity.
- Experiential learning creates a productive classroom environment and a positive attitude. These experiences make class time different, fun, and exciting.
- These experiences link students to the Jewish tradition of learning in order to do; they model the ways we hope that our students will live their Jewish lives.

USING TECHNOLOGY

Your students use technology in their daily lives, at home and at school, whether it's through a computer, iPad, or smart phone. There are infinite ways you can take advantage of the Internet and digital applications to deepen understanding, reinforce concepts, share learning with families, and add creativity, interactivity, and excitement to your lessons. Suggestions are provided throughout this book for ways to use technology to enrich your lessons. Search the video collection at www.teachparentstech.org to sharpen your computer skills, and recommend the site to parents as well.

The Behrman House Online Learning Center

One way to take advantage of technology is to create a Jewish Identity class Web site or blog through the Behrman House Online Learning Center. Find multimedia resources, simplify class preparation, share assignments and reminders with students, organize project-based learning activities, extend class time with at-home practice, and much more. Learn about the OLC here: www.behrmanhouse.com/discover-the-online-learning-center.

The Building Jewish Identity Digital Companion

Enrich your lessons with this multimedia supplement to the *Building Jewish Identity* textbooks. The pages of the book come alive with videos, interactive games and activities, a digital sketchpad, and other tools and resources. Download it free here: www.behrmanhouse.com/building-jewish-identity.

Creating a Class Blog

A class blog encourages students to share their work and creates an ongoing record of their ideas and accomplishments. It can effectively increase contact time between school and home, and it offers an opportunity for families to be engaged by the curriculum of the class. Inviting parents to read their child's posts can open doors and dialogue between school and home, can further the conversation at home, and can encourage parents to learn more on the subject themselves.

A blog can also help you assess student learning and help students share ideas that they might be reluctant, or lack time, to share during in-class discussion. You can even use it to create a class yearbook at the end of the year.

Use the Behrman House Online Learning Center or check out Google's free tool www.blogger.com to get started. If you use www.blogger.com, be sure to set the access controls so that your blog can only be accessed by the class.

TEACHING STRATEGIES

Interpersonal and Intrapersonal Learners

Some students learn best through interaction with others (interpersonal), while others learn best independently (intrapersonal). With this in mind, there are suggestions in the lesson plans for independent work and for activities and discussions with a study partner, group, or the whole class. If the activity does not specify that students should meet with a partner or group, plan to involve the whole class.

Group Work

All of the lessons include opportunities for group work. Whenever possible, plan ahead for how you will form working groups. It is important to vary the composition of working groups. For some tasks you will want to group students with a variety of skills and interests. For others, you might choose to group students with similar skills together. Consider factors such as gender balance, widening social groups, and the academic and social needs of all students. The choices you make about group assignments have the potential to reassure students that they will be successful and let them know that you understand who they are.

Group work can be very rewarding and is most successful when each group member knows his or her specific responsibilities. To help clarify the group's task, prepare written instructions before class. You may want to create laminated index cards to distribute that describe the tasks of group members. Some possible roles include the following:

- Recorder—records the group's suggestions or findings
- Reporter—reports the group's work to the class
- Illustrator—draws the group's ideas to present to the class
- Investigator—researches to discover information
- Encourager—encourages group members to stay on task
- Reader—reads information aloud to the group

BEING INCLUSIVE

Children vary in their learning styles. Some students learn best with a hands-on approach, while others learn best through a visual or auditory approach. In general, teachers who present material in many different ways will be able to reach many more students. This Lesson Plan Manual reflects a variety of learning styles. The suggestions that follow will help ensure success for all students:

- After a narrative is read, rephrase and paraphrase the content to emphasize important points. Review vocabulary and post key words for visual learners and future reference. Ask questions to clarify points of potential misunderstanding, and invite students to do the same.
- Where Hebrew is used, pronounce words slowly, break them into syllables, and have students repeat after you. Ask for the assistance of a Hebrew staff member or your education director if you need Hebrew practice.
- Allow students to be flexible in creative tasks and adapt those tasks when needed. Some students paint best with words, and others create a song more easily than a sentence.

Teachers of students with special needs have additional challenges. These children may have a broad range of cognitive, neurological, physical, and behavioral disabilities that impact learning. It is always helpful to find out from parents or guardians about the accommodations made for their children in secular school. The following are suggestions for students with learning, perceptual, or attention problems:

- For students with attention deficit and auditory processing problems, teach in small increments, and present one instruction at a time. Ask students to repeat the instruction to make sure they have processed it.
- For students with attention deficit problems, limit teaching segments to 10–15 minutes, and allow for movement between activities.
- For students with decoding problems, make flashcards with a few key words. Students can take them home and practice reading them with their parents or guardians. Keep a shoe box of flashcards for students who need them. Provide opportunities for choral reading rather than asking students to read aloud individually.
- For students with attention deficit and visual figure-ground problems, mask parts of the page so they can see only the section that is being worked on.
- For students with fine motor and handwriting problems, limit the amount of writing, drawing, and cutting that is required. You or an assistant may perform the more difficult parts of a project and allow the student to finish the task.

BUILDING JEWISH IDENTITY

PART 1
Lesson Plans for Volume 1: Our Community

OUR COMMUNITY
CHAPTER 1: Jewish Like Me

LESSON 1

In what ways is my Jewish identity similar to others?

Lesson Objectives: Students will be able to:
1. Explain that Jewish people share common elements of identity.
2. Explain that being Jewish means different things to different people.
3. Cite ways that their Jewish identity is similar to, as well as different from, that of others.

Materials Needed: Graham crackers, small marshmallows, chocolate bars, enlarged copies of photos and quotes from pages 4–5, tape, sticky notes, pencils

Getting Started: (10 minutes)
Before class, set out plates with graham crackers, marshmallows, and pieces of chocolate bars. When students enter, ask them to identify what these items together create *(s'mores)*. How were they able to recognize the identity of the combination of ingredients? *(They recognized its parts.)*

Say the blessing for cake (*Baruch Atah Adonai Eloheinu Melech ha'olam, borei minei mizonot/* Praised are You, Adonai our God, Ruler of the world, who creates different kinds of food). As students snack, explain that Jewish people also share parts of their identities. What are the common ingredients of the students' Jewish identities? *(They belong to the same synagogue, can recite the* alef bet, *know common vocabulary words.)*

Exploring the Text:
1. (10 minutes) On each set of photos and quotes from **pages 4–5**, write "I am like (person's name), when I …" Tape the photos and quotes around the room. Distribute sticky notes and pencils to each student, and ask them to rotate through the gallery of interviews, choosing two or three subjects who are most like themselves. Have students complete the sentence "I am like … when I …" on sticky notes, attaching the notes to the photos. To conclude, lead students on a tour of the photo gallery, emphasizing the different ways that they saw themselves in the interviews.
2. **Experiential Learning:** (25 minutes) Pass out paper and invite students to draw their self-portraits—pictures that describe their own Jewish identities *(baking for Shabbat, participating in a tzedakah project)*. Have each student present his or her portrait to the class, and mention some similarities and differences among the portraits. Display the portraits to create a class Jewish identity art gallery.

Wrapping It Up: (5 minutes) Ask students to name one aspect of their Jewish identities that they share with classmates and name one aspect in which they differ.

The Tech Connection: Use your Online Learning Center classroom space or a class blog (see the Introduction) to create a chart of Jewish activities. Have students check off the activities in which they have engaged *(for example, lighting Ḥanukkah candles, giving tzedakah)*. Once all students have completed their entries, announce the most common activities for students in the class.

OUR COMMUNITY

CHAPTER 1: LESSON 2

What are unique parts of my Jewish identity?

Lesson Objectives: Students will be able to:
1. Cite ways that being Jewish impacts their lives.
2. Explain the meaning of their Hebrew names.
3. Explain that we each express our Jewish selves in personal ways.

Materials Needed: Index cards, pencils, markers, templates or stencils of Hebrew letters, brown kraft paper (butcher paper)

Getting Started: (5 minutes)
Label pairs of index cards with statements of common Jewish activities (for example, I can recite the Sh'ma, I give tzedakah). Give each student a card, and ask students to find the person with the matching card. Have partners talk about their shared activity. Is it something they do often? Can it be done in different ways? What is the best thing about it? Have each pair share with another pair of students.

Exploring the Text:
1. (15 minutes) Ask students to turn to **Jewish Me** (page 6), explaining that they will have an opportunity to think about the unique parts of their Jewish lives. Have students complete their image boards on **pages 6–7**. Students might create illustrations and use key words or phrases. Point out that Jewish activities can include what they read, listen to, eat, and think or talk about. (Save the image boards so you can revisit them at the end of the school year, in chapter 7.)

2. (10 minutes) Explain that our Hebrew names are part of our Jewish identities. In advance of this lesson, have students ask their families about their names and find out whether they were named after a family member, who else in the family might share that name, and the meaning or origin of their Hebrew or English names. In the classroom, ask students to form a circle and share what they have discovered. Prompt each student to create a poster about his or her name and share that with the class. Add Hebrew names to the class blog or Online Learning Center classroom space.

3. **Experiential Learning:** (15 minutes) Divide the class into groups of three to four students. Have one student in each group lie down on the kraft paper and the other students draw an outline of the body onto the paper. Ask the students to list their Jewish activities on the appropriate body part on the paper, such as listening to Jewish music on the ears and saying prayers or eating ḥallah on the mouth. Each student group then cuts out each paper body and introduces it to the other student groups, comparing their Jewish activities. Display the paper people in a class gallery.

Wrapping It Up: (5 minutes) Ask one student to name a Jewish activity. The second student repeats the name of the previous activity and adds his or her own. The third student repeats the name of the two previous activities and adds one to the list. Repeat until all students have participated. The last student will have a comprehensive list of Jewish activities!

The Tech Connection: Help students search the Internet for information on their Hebrew and/or English names, such as their meanings and whether anyone famous has the name.

OUR COMMUNITY

CHAPTER 2: Pieces of the Puzzle: Jewish Community LESSON 1

How do I contribute to my Jewish community?

Lesson Objectives: Students will be able to:
1. Explain that our identity is formed by being part of numerous communities.
2. Express how they are committed to being part of the Jewish community.
3. Cite ways they might participate in the Jewish community in the future.

Materials Needed: Pencils, markers, magazines, poster board, scissors, colorful sticky notes, adhesive stars

Getting Started: (10 minutes)
Ask students to form a large circle. Tell them that their circle represents the community that is your class, one of the communities to which they each belong. Now ask that they form circles by town of residence. Form new circles according to their secular schools. Create smaller communities based on sports or instruments they play or camps they attend. Summarize by pointing out that each community offers us a chance to develop a part of our total identity; for example, a student might be a Jewish tuba-playing ballet dancer who attends X school or a Jewish Spanish-speaking speed-swimming Boy Scout who attends Y school. Ask students to share something they have in common with other members of their Jewish community.

Exploring the Text:
1. (5 minutes) Ask three students to each read one of the paragraphs in **Meet Amalya** (page 9). As students are reading, prompt other students to underline the ways that Amalya shows her commitment to the Jewish community. Ask students to share their underlined statements and lead them in a discussion of how Amalya might manage her various activities.
2. (15 minutes) Using Amalya's experiences as the example, ask students to identify three ways they show their commitment to the Jewish community (for example, singing in the choir). Form groups within the class according to student activities. Each group creates a poster of its commitments, using their own artwork, combined with images from the Internet or magazines. Create a poster gallery entitled "Our Jewish Communities" using the work of each group.
3. **Experiential Learning:** (15 minutes) Tell the narrative **Synagogue Central** (page 10). Emphasize that the synagogue is a place that helps us to develop our Jewish identities. Distribute sticky notes to students. Have them walk throughout the synagogue, writing on their sticky notes the activities they see going on or represented (in signs, notices, etc.). Back in the classroom, instruct students to use their sticky notes to create a class collage. Ask them to write their names on activities in which they already engage and to place stars on the activities they would like to do in the future.

Wrapping It Up: (5 minutes) Students take turns completing the following statement: "In the future, I would like to further participate in my Jewish community by …"

The Tech Connection: On your Online Learning Center classroom space or the class blog, have students write about the synagogue activities they discovered. They might invite parents to comment about their own experiences participating in these, or other, activities.

OUR COMMUNITY

CHAPTER 2: LESSON 2

How does diversity contribute to the Jewish community?

Lesson Objectives: Students will be able to:
1. Explain that communities require many types of participation by their members.
2. Cite some of the diversity within their local Jewish communities.
3. Explain the importance of diversity in the Jewish community.

Materials Needed: Unlined index cards, world map, pushpins, pictures of geographically diverse synagogues (labeled with the country name); recipes, ingredients, and equipment for Sephardi ḥaroset

Getting Started: (10 minutes)
Assign students to small groups. Ask them to name the roles people take in local Jewish communities: the school *(principal, teacher)*, synagogue *(rabbi, cantor)*, and Jewish community center *(athletic director, someone who plans classes, arts and crafts instructor)*. Prompt them to think about the buildings, worship, learning, membership, and so on. Solicit responses and create a master list on the board.

Exploring the Text:
1. (15 minutes) Ask each group to select three roles from the master list. Using unlined index cards, students complete a card similar to those in **Inside the Synagogue** (page 11) for each role. Then, each group writes and performs a short skit that brings together the three roles *(a school seder, a Shabbat service, a holiday celebration)*. Emphasize the diversity of participation that a Jewish community requires—and the diversity the students just demonstrated in this activity (for example, someone may have done the writing, another acting).
2. (5 minutes) Distribute a synagogue photograph to each student and ask that he or she mark the location of the assigned synagogue on the map with a pushpin. In what ways do students think the members of these synagogues might differ from members of others? In what ways are members of *Am Yisrael* one people?
3. **Experiential Learning:** (15 minutes) As you set out ingredients and recipes for ḥaroset, explain that Jewish food traditions are often influenced by geography. People ate what was easily available. Ask students what ḥaroset ingredients they are familiar with (most students are probably familiar with Ashkenazi (European) traditions, and their ḥaroset ingredients will be apple-based). Tell them that your tasting will take you to another part of the Jewish world—Sepharad (the countries around the Mediterranean and Spain).
4. Divide students into groups, providing ingredients for each to cut. Combine ingredients; say the blessing *(Baruch Atah Adonai Eloheinu Melech ha'olam, borei p'ri ha'eitz*/Praised are You, Adonai our God, Ruler of the world, who creates the fruit of the tree) and enjoy. Ask students how Sephardi ḥaroset differs from the one to which they are accustomed and what might account for the difference *(figs and dates grow in warm climates)*. What do all types of ḥaroset have in common? *(We eat it on Passover as a symbol of the mortar used by Jewish slaves.)*

Wrapping It Up: (5 minutes) Have students explore diversity within their own classroom and school community by interviewing each other and several teachers about where their families come from and whether their families are Ashkenazi or Sephardi.

The Tech Connection: Search Google for a world map and for recipes for Sephardi ḥaroset. Include recipes on your Online Learning Center classroom space or the class blog.

OUR COMMUNITY

CHAPTER 3: A Rich Heritage: History and Stories   LESSON 1

How can stories teach us about the Jewish people and about ourselves?

Lesson Objectives: Students will be able to:
1. Explain that stories teach us lessons about our people.
2. Define *brit* as a covenant and cite as an example the relationship of Abraham and God.
3. Illustrate how learning from our stories helps us to create a Jewish community.

Materials Needed: A variety of books, including a Ḥumash (printed Torah), paper, markers, pencils, poster board

Getting Started: (5 minutes)
Display a variety of books (for example, cookbook, phone book, comic book, prayer book). Ask students to propose ideas for why we might use each. Add a Ḥumash. Ask the students for what purposes we might use it *(reading stories or learning about what is important to the Jewish people)*.

Exploring the Text:
1. (15 minutes) Use the introductory narrative as a preface to telling **The Power of a Story** (page 14). Have students work in groups to retell the lesson of the story—that we can turn our flaws into strengths. Ask that each group consider creative ways to tell the story, such as a print advertisement, a poem, a jingle, or a T-shirt slogan (for example, "Always find the best in you!").

2. (10 minutes) Introduce **Turning to the Torah** (page 16) as a source of our people's stories. Read the text Genesis 17:4, 17:7–9 as a class, checking for understanding as the text is read. Have students work in ḥevruta (study partner groups) to answer the questions about God and Abraham. Ask student volunteers to share answers with the class.

3. (5 minutes) Using **Words to Know** (page 17), define *brit*. Ask: Why would someone (or God) wish to enter into a *brit*? Why might a class want to be bound by a *brit*? *(To help everyone share an understanding of what it means to be a class member, to help solve problems and avoid conflicts.)*

4. **Experiential Learning:** (10 minutes) Divide the class into small groups. Ask each group to think about a class issue that could be resolved by the creation of a *brit (for example, some students prefer not to read Hebrew aloud in front of the class, but students need to practice aloud to improve skills)*. Ask one student to explain the issue and another to indicate the needs of the first party to the *brit*. Another student presents the needs of the second party to the *brit*. Other students propose various solutions *(for example, students might read aloud in small groups, volunteer when confident, or read into a recorder)*.

Wrapping It Up: (5 minutes) Ask students to create a Six Word Story that summarizes something they learned from this lesson *("I can be the best me"; "A brit means we all understand")*.

The Tech Connection: Google "Six Word Stories" to learn more about their history and use in the classroom. Add the students' stories from **Wrapping It Up** to your Online Learning Center classroom space or the class blog.

OUR COMMUNITY — CHAPTER 3: LESSON 2

How are new stories of Am Yisrael added to our people's treasury of stories?

Lesson Objectives: Students will be able to:
1. Explain that objects, foods, and rituals evoke personal and historical memories.
2. Define Diaspora and identify some communities where Jews live or have lived outside of Israel.
3. Share some of their own Jewish memories and explain how our stories connect us to each other.

Materials Needed: Memory-evoking items and pictures, world map, masking tape, string, scissors, paper strips; staplers, tape, or glue sticks

Getting Started: (5 minutes)
Ask student volunteers to select from a collection of items and pictures (for example, a birthday candle, a baseball, a Jewish food or ritual object). Have students share a personal story that their chosen item evokes.

Exploring the Text:
1. (15 minutes) Read the story **Adding New Chapters** (page 18) as a class, with students seated on the floor close together. Ask students to imagine they were there. What was it like? Why were you so happy? What was it like on that plane? Why did you kiss the ground when you landed in Israel? Ask students what symbol they might add to their families' seder to remind them of Mazi's story.

2. (10 minutes) Write the word "Diaspora" on the board, and read **My Heart Is in the East** (page 20) aloud. Ask students to do the exercise **Identifying Diaspora Communities** (page 21). Have students unscramble the names of the Diaspora communities and then form nine groups, representing each Diaspora community. Using string and masking tape, with a world map as their background, ask students to connect "their" Diaspora community with Jerusalem. Which way would people in that community have faced to look toward Jerusalem? Ask students to imagine they are standing in "their" community and face Jerusalem. What are they thinking?

3. **Experiential Learning:** (15 minutes) Ask students to think of two or three Jewish stories (for example, personal memories, or stories from the Bible, Jewish history, or the great teachers on **page 22**) and briefly write or sketch each on a paper strip. Have students share a story with a partner and join their strips, making links, and then share a story with another pair of students and link strips. Repeat until all paper chains have been linked together. Emphasize the joy of sharing stories, and hang the class community story chain in the classroom.

Wrapping It Up: (5 minutes) Ask students to stand in a circle, with each student adding a three-word memory related to Jewish history or holidays (*Grandma frying latkes, booing Haman's name, jam on matzah, freedom from Egypt*). See how often the verbal chain of memory can wrap around the class.

The Tech Connection: Use your Online Learning Center classroom space or the class blog to have students share their stories with their families.

OUR COMMUNITY
CHAPTER 4: Speaking the Same Language: Hebrew LESSON 1

How does praying in Hebrew help create Jewish community?

Lesson Objectives: Students will be able to:
1. Identify Hebrew as our language of prayer and explain its importance in building community.
2. Demonstrate the universality of our Hebrew liturgy using the Sh'ma as an example.
3. Explain the source of the mitzvah to hang *mezuzot*, locate it in the V'ahavta, and recognize what all *mezuzot* share.

Materials Needed: Copies of the Sh'ma headed "This is the Sh'ma in . . ." (each completed with the name of one of five countries), recordings of Sh'ma melodies (from the cantor or online sources), copies of Deuteronomy 6:4–9 (English/Hebrew), copies of the Sh'ma and V'ahavta from your congregation's prayer book (English/Hebrew), mezuzah parchment(s), unlined index cards, pencils, fine-point markers

Getting Started: (5 minutes)
Divide students into five groups, each group representing a country. Tell students they are all members of *Am Yisrael*, and give each group copies of the Sh'ma marked for their country. Ask that students all recite the Sh'ma at once. Ask: What allows Jews representing different nations and languages to pray together? *(The words are the same; the language of prayer is the same for all of them.)* How does that feel?

Exploring the Text:
1. (10 minutes) Relate the narrative **The Language of Our Past, Present, and Future** (page 25). Play a selection of Sh'ma melodies that are different from the one with which your students are familiar. Point out that the words in each of the versions are in Hebrew, our shared language of prayer. The melodies might be different, but the identical text makes us feel like a member of every Jewish community. Teach a melody of the Sh'ma that is new to your class.

2. (10 minutes) Point students to **Words to Know** (page 25), and remind them that *mezuzah* (pl. *mezuzot*) means "doorposts" in Hebrew and also refers to the object that we place on our doorposts. Point out the mezuzah on the doorposts of your classroom or synagogue. Give each student a copy of Deuteronomy 6:4–9, a copy of the Sh'ma and V'ahavta from the prayer book, and a copy of a mezuzah parchment. Ask students to find the word *mezuzot* in each of these texts. Which text originates the commandment? *(Torah)* Which is the reminder? *(V'ahavta)* And which is used to fulfill the commandment? *(mezuzah parchment)* How is each teaching important?

3. **Experiential Learning:** (20 minutes) Give each student unlined index cards and a pencil. Take the class on a brief "mezuzah hunt" around the synagogue or school hallway. Have students find the element common to each *(the shin, which stands for Shaddai, one of God's names)*. Ask each student to sketch a favorite mezuzah. Return to class and ask that students color or otherwise decorate their mezuzah. Display drawings in the classroom.

Wrapping It Up: (5 minutes) Ask students to cite ways in which Hebrew makes them feel part of the Jewish community *(we use the same language for prayer anywhere in the world, Jews all over the world mark our homes with mezuzot)*.

The Tech Connection: Visit www.youtube.com to listen to versions of the Sh'ma.

OUR COMMUNITY

CHAPTER 4: LESSON 2

How does using Hebrew help us form our Jewish identity?

Lesson Objectives: Students will be able to:
1. Explain the importance of a people and a country sharing a common language.
2. Describe the work of Eliezer Ben-Yehuda in creating the modern Hebrew language.
3. Cite some of the modern Hebrew words they know.

Materials Needed: Paper, pencils, sticky notes

Getting Started: (5 minutes)

Using the graphic on **page 24**, ask students to select a version of "hello" that they can pronounce. Have them simultaneously say "hello" to class members. Then have them simultaneously say "hello" in Hebrew (*shalom*). Ask students to compare the two experiences *(one felt confusing, one sounded familiar and comfortable)*.

Exploring the Text:
1. (10 minutes) Briefly tell the story of the tower of Babel, from **The Importance of a Common Language** (page 24). Divide students into teams, and give them 5 minutes to build a tower with any building materials they can find in the room, but without any talking, not even to plan their tower. Discuss how it felt.

2. (10 minutes) Ask students to read the narrative **An Ancient Language Blooms Again** (page 26) and call out adjectives describing Eliezer Ben-Yehuda. How was his idea challenging? *(How do you speak a language that no one knows? How do you get other people to agree to do it?)* How was it amazing? *(It helped people to feel proud of having their own language; it helped to form a nation.)*

3. (15 minutes) Divide the class into several teams. Give each team 3 minutes to brainstorm a list of Hebrew words whose English translations they know, including words from the sanctuary, holiday vocabulary, and words taken from English (for example, pizza [*pitza*], telephone [*telefon*]). Once the lists have been completed, each team in turn offers a Hebrew word and its translation. Other teams have to cross that word off their lists. The team that has any words left at the conclusion of the game is declared the *m'natzei'aḥ* (winner).

4. **Experiential Learning:** (10 minutes) Have students do the activity **Hebrew Lessons** (page 29) and select three of the Hebrew words from the puzzle to use at home. Have students practice their words with one another, then write their chosen words on sticky notes to post and teach at home. Ask that they report back on their, and their family's, learning in the next class period.

Wrapping It Up: (5 minutes) Ask students to complete the following sentence: "Knowing how to speak *Ivrit* (Hebrew) is *magniv* (cool) because …"

The Tech Connection: Search Google for "Hebrew sign maker" to type Hebrew words to post in the classroom. Add the answers from **Wrapping It Up** to the class Online Learning Center space or blog.

OUR COMMUNITY

CHAPTER 5: Learning by Doing: Symbols and Rituals — LESSON 1

What are symbols, and how do symbols help us remember?

Lesson Objectives: Students will be able to:
1. Explain the meaning and use of a symbol.
2. Explain that we can understand new symbols of our shared culture.
3. Create a new holiday symbol and explain its meaning.

Materials Needed: American flag, team logos, brand symbols, Israeli flag, paper, pencils, a bunch of scallions, a pomegranate, air-hardening clay

Getting Started: (5 minutes)
Arrange a display of the flags, logos, and brand symbols. Ask students what these items have in common *(they are symbols)*. Have students define the word "symbol" *(a representation of some information)*. Focusing on the American flag, ask students what the stars and stripes represent. How did they know the answers? *(They are part of the culture in which the flag is a symbol.)*

Exploring the Text:
1. (10 minutes) Displaying the Israeli flag, share **How the Flag Got Its Star and Stripes** (page 30). Emphasize that our American and our Jewish cultures have two different stars and stripes stories and we share in both stories. Have students read **Identifying Jewish Symbols** (page 31). Ask students to underline the definition of a symbol and to circle how a symbol "works." Ask them to select one of the symbols pictured and share a personal story of that symbol with another student.

2. (10 minutes) Tell students that some Sephardi Jews (from the Middle East) use scallions at their seder table. Wave the scallions in a whipping motion. Ask students why they think scallions might be a Passover symbol *(they remind us of the Jewish slaves being beaten with whips)*. Cut open the pomegranate, and tell students that some Sephardi Jews use the pomegranate at Rosh Hashanah because it has so many seeds. What do students think that the large number of seeds might represent at the start of a new year? *(lots of good luck, a lot of good wishes)* Ask students how they knew what these symbols represented *(the memory of having been a slave and extending good wishes are important ideas in our culture)*.

3. **Experiential Learning:** (20 minutes) Ask students to select their favorite holiday and to think of a personal story about that holiday. What might be an appropriate symbol to represent their story? Ask students to create it using air-hardening clay. Ask students to share their symbols and stories with each other.

Wrapping It Up: (5 minutes) Ask students to share ideas on how symbols are like books *(they contain information and stories)*. How are they like foods? *(They engage our senses.)* What else are they like? Why are symbols important? How are they fun?

The Tech Connection: Use your Online Learning Center classroom space or the class blog to have students share stories about their symbols with their families.

OUR COMMUNITY

CHAPTER 5: LESSON 2

How do objects signify and beautify our rituals?

Lesson Objectives: Students will be able to:
1. Explain the importance of objects in the performance of rituals.
2. Define the concept of *hidur mitzvah.*
3. Design a ritual object that expresses their understanding of ritual objects as creative expressions of Jewish ritual.

Materials Needed: Plain *kippot*, fabric markers, other craft embellishments, string, clothespins

Getting Started: (5 minutes)
Ask students to think of an item that is precious to them. How do they demonstrate that they consider the item to be valued? *(They keep it in a special place; they treat it with care.)* What makes the item precious? *(It was a gift from someone special; it is beautiful or expensive, or they just love it.)*

Exploring the Text:
1. (5 minutes) As a class, read **A Hands-On Tradition** (page 32), and ask students to do the activity **Holiday-Style**. Ask students to think about rituals as small scenes in which we act out what is important to us *(on Passover, the symbols on the seder plate help us to act out an important story; the dreidel helps us to remember miracles)*. What are these objects, and how are they important? *(They are the props we use to perform rituals.)*

2. (5 minutes) Read the narrative **The Art of the Ritual** (page 36), asking students to underline how we show that ritual items are important to us *(made from the best materials, beautiful, artists put their own unique stamp on them)*. Ask students to define *hidur mitzvah* (*the practice of enhancing our celebrations with beautiful ritual objects*). Ask what makes a ritual object beautiful in addition to being made of fine materials *(a lot of care went into making it; it helps us do mitzvot and remember Jewish times of our lives)*.

3. **Experiential Learning:** (25 minutes) Take students to the sanctuary or to view cabinets where ritual objects are displayed. Prompt students to notice items that look modern or old-fashioned, as well as the variety of styles for an object (for example, head coverings), and any identifying information (for example, national symbols on flags, sports themes or cartoon characters on a *ḥanukkiyah*, bar mitzvah information on a *kippah*). Return to class and ask students how individual creativity can be seen in Jewish ritual objects *(materials, styles, interests)*. Have students complete **Your Turn** (page 37), then explain that they're each going to create a *kippah* that demonstrates *hidur mitzvah*. After students sketch their design, distribute plain *kippot*, fabric markers, and craft supplies. Create a Kippah Gallery in the classroom for a week or two, and then send them home for students to use or give to family members.

Wrapping It Up: (5 minutes) Have each student contribute a phrase to the following sentence: "We make mitzvot beautiful when we …"

The Tech Connection: Search the Internet for images that students might want to use as reference in creating their designs. Use your Online Learning Center classroom space or the class blog to post pictures of the class Kippah Gallery.

OUR COMMUNITY

CHAPTER 6: Becoming Our Best Selves: Mitzvot — LESSON 1

How do mitzvot help us to build our best possible community?

Lesson Objectives: Students will be able to:
1. Cite and explain the pillars of Judaism *(Torah learning, worship of God, acts of loving-kindness)*.
2. Define the two categories of mitzvot *(between people, between people and God)*.
3. Explain and demonstrate their understanding of what it means to love one's neighbor.

Materials Needed: Chalk (one piece per student), three large poster boards, markers

Getting Started: (5 minutes)
Write the words "The Best Day Possible" on the board. As students enter the classroom, ask each to write their ideas of what constitutes the Best Day Possible under the heading. Review responses as a class to see what their ideas have in common *(how we treat one another, accomplishments, treats)*.

Exploring the Text:
1. (15 minutes) In advance, label three poster boards as follows: Torah (learning), Worship of God, and Acts of Loving-Kindness. Write the verse from Pirkei Avot (**Mitzvot Build Community**, page 38) on the blackboard. What are pillars? What do they do? Have students discuss the text with a neighbor. How do they understand the text? *(Pillars hold something up and make it sturdy and strong; these particular pillars help the world be a good place.)* Ask one student from each pair to report back to the class about their conversation.

2. Ask students how they build the three pillars in their own lives. Hang the three pillar posters, and ask that students circulate among them, writing down actions that they do in each category. Summarize the actions as being mitzvot/commandments. Ask that students return to the pillars and indicate whether their mitzvot were between people or between people and God by putting a P or a G in front of each of their actions. Why is each category of mitzvot important? *(Each helps our community to come together and be strong.)*

3. (5 minutes) Read **The Importance of Caring** (page 40), and ask students to answer the questions. Review suggestions of how we can be fair and kind to others.

4. **Experiential Learning:** (20 minutes) Divide the class into groups. Using their ideas for ways to love your neighbor as yourself, ask that each group create a skit that demonstrates one or more of these ideas. Have groups act out their skits, and then discuss how the actions in each skit help build community.

Wrapping It Up: (5 minutes) Ask students to commit to one new idea for demonstrating caring, fairness, and kindness in the coming week.

The Tech Connection: With students' permission, record the skits and post them to your Online Learning Center classroom space or the class blog. Invite parents to comment. Ask students to post a description of their experience during the week in demonstrating fairness and kindness in some new way.

OUR COMMUNITY
CHAPTER 6: LESSON 2

How can doing mitzvot help us to be our best selves?

Lesson Objectives: Students will be able to:
1. Define *tikun olam* and their personal *tikun olam* personalities.
2. Explain how their *tikun olam* personalities can impact their choices of *tikun olam* projects.
3. Demonstrate how they will bring their skills and interests to a class plan.

Materials Needed: Four pieces of construction paper (marked A, B, C, or D), slips of paper (marked A, B, C, or D—enough slips of paper to have four per student), paper, markers, pencils

Getting Started: (5 minutes)
Set the following scene: School is closed due to a water-main break. Ask: What will you do with the extra time that you have? Have students brainstorm a list of possibilities *(play sports, watch TV, see friends, read, enjoy art or music)*. Record them on the board. What do students notice? *(a variety of activities, ranging from active to quiet, social or solitary)* Ask students what the variety of choices says about people *(everyone has their own style; no choice is right or wrong)*.

Exploring the Text:
1. (5 minutes) Read **Your *Tikun Olam* Personality** (page 42), asking that students underline the verb phrases in each example of fixing the world *(look out for, take care of, work to build, speak out for)*. Emphasize the different ways that people choose to help fix the world.

2. (15 minutes) Place signs A, B, C, and D in different corners of the room. In each area, have slips of paper marked with the corresponding letter. Read to the students the first question and the first set of responses in **What's Your Way of Changing the World?** (page 43). Ask students to consider the responses and go to the sign (A, B, C, or D) that best represents what they would do. At the sign, each student takes the corresponding slip of paper. Repeat for the other three questions. Have students return to their seats and sort their slips of paper. Refer to **If You Answered …** (page 43) to determine students' *tikun olam* personalities.

3. **Experiential Learning:** (20 minutes) Propose one or more organizations or projects that students might support through active engagement (for example, visits, letter writing, collecting items to donate). Have students select the project they wish to adopt. Ask each student to cite a way that they will support the project, and have students group according to their ideas (the letter writers, the item collectors, and so on). Have each group begin their specific plan, indicating what they will do and what they need to make it happen. Collect student input, and allocate time to assist the class in getting their projects started.

Wrapping It Up: (5 minutes) Ask students to complete the following sentence: "Doing *tikun olam* helps us to …"

The Tech Connection: Use your Online Learning Center classroom space or the class blog to have students post *tikun olam* project plans, enlist parental assistance, and track the project's progress.

OUR COMMUNITY

CHAPTER 7: Your Jewish Identity

LESSON 1

How do I say Hineni! *(Here I am!) to the Jewish community?*

Lesson Objectives: Students will be able to:

1. Cite some of the components of their Jewish lives.
2. Express their Jewish thoughts and ideas.
3. Share their Jewish questions and respond to those of other students.

Materials Needed: One large cube-shaped gift box per student, markers, glue, embellishments (e.g., glitter, colored paper), scissors, paper, pencils, timer

Getting Started: (5 minutes)

Ask students to complete the **Checklist** (page 47) or make their own list of Jewish experiences they have tried for the first time this year. Then have them turn back to the section **Jewish Me** (pages 6–7) that they completed at the beginning of the course. Ask students to name something new they learned this year about their Jewish identity.

Exploring the Text:

1. (25 minutes) Distribute a box to each student, and explain that they will create a Jewish Identity Box—using words, symbols, poems, illustrations, and/or decorations—using the sides of their box as a canvas. Students should brainstorm subjects they might want to depict (for example, Jewish things they love, questions they have, symbols, stories, pictures of family members, summer camp mementos, and anything else they believe is important to their Jewish identities). After the boxes are decorated, encourage students to bring them home and fill them with pictures and personal "artifacts" of their Jewish lives (for example, a picture of their favorite Jewish book, a bar mitzvah invitation, a program in which they participated, a dreidel).

2. **Experiential Learning:** (15 minutes) Divide students into groups of three to four students. Ask each student to share an artifact of their Jewish lives with their group. Then ask them to share questions they have about Judaism and about being Jewish. Encourage other group members to respond and to ask their own questions. If possible, invite the rabbi, education director, or parents to an upcoming class to respond to unanswered questions and to see students' projects.

Wrapping It Up: (5 minutes) Ask each student to complete the following sentence: "The most amazing thing about my Jewish self is …" The results might create the heading of a bulletin board or display, with boxes put on view.

The Tech Connection: Use your Online Learning Center classroom space or the class blog to post photos of students' boxes, along with the sentence completions from **Wrapping It Up.** You can also use this space to respond to unanswered questions or ask students to respond.

BUILDING JEWISH IDENTITY

PART 2
Lesson Plans for Volume 2: Sacred Time: The Jewish Calendar and Life Cycle

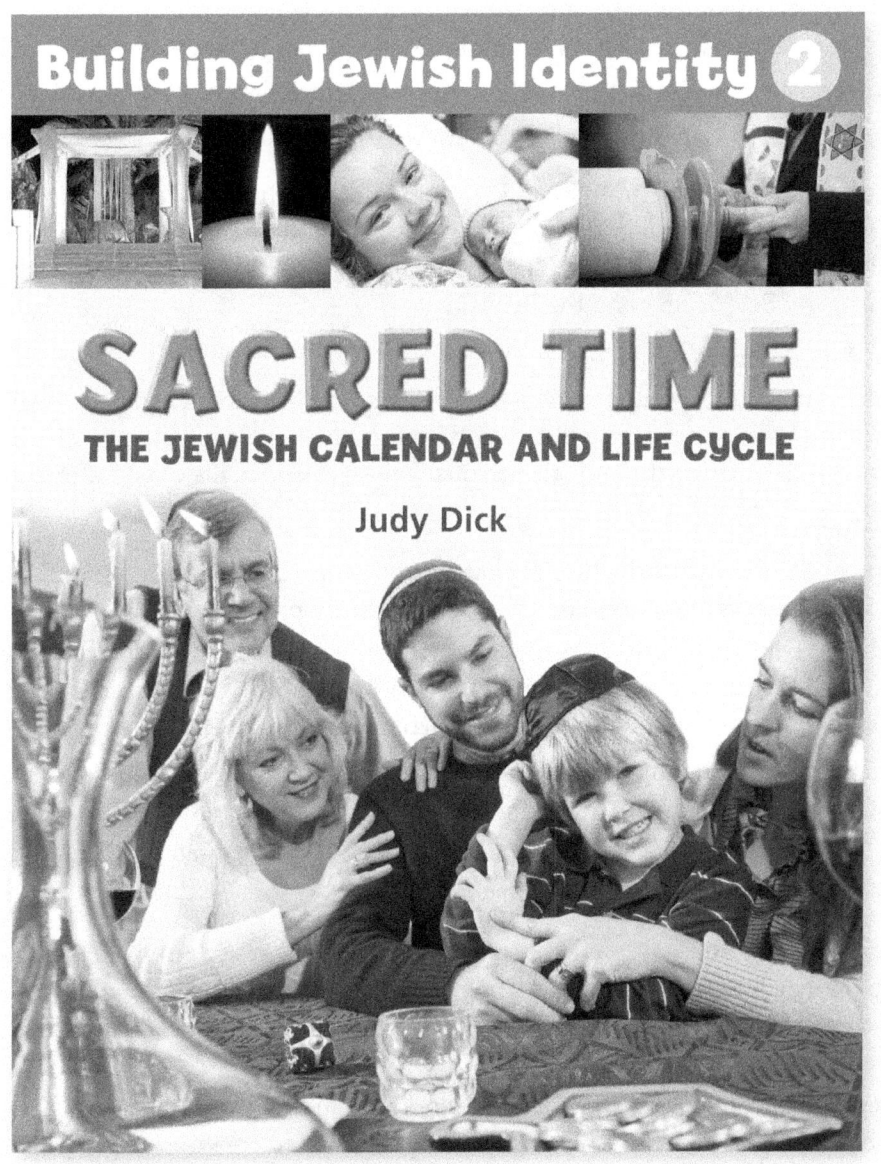

SACRED TIME: THE JEWISH CALENDAR AND LIFE CYCLE
CHAPTER 1: Times of Your Life LESSON 1

What are the times of a Jewish life?

Lesson Objectives: Students will be able to:
1. Explain that the Jewish people share a unique calendar of holidays and life-cycle events.
2. Compare and contrast the annual calendar of Jewish observances with the calendar of a Jewish life.
3. Cite examples of Jewish observances that they have shared.

Materials Needed: Items or pictures related to telling time, including watches, clocks, sundials, monthly and annual calendars; sets of index cards with one Jewish holiday name per card; sets of index cards with one Jewish life-cycle event per card; file folders; paper; markers; (optional) CD or video of the song "Turn, Turn, Turn," by Pete Seeger and the Byrds

Getting Started: (5 minutes)
Display all the items or pictures related to telling time. Ask students to think about all the ways that we tell time (the school week/year, sunrise to sunset, twenty-four hours). Explain that Jews tell time all of those ways and add two others—the Jewish year and our personal Jewish calendar, the calendar of the Jewish life cycle.

Exploring the Text:
1. (5 minutes) Read the **Introductory Narrative** and **Appreciating Every Minute** (pages 4–5) as a class. Have students respond to the questions in study partner groups.
2. (10 minutes) Divide students into groups, and give each group a set of holiday index cards. Ask that they put the cards in order (beginning with Tu BiShevat). Have students write a sentence describing what each holiday signifies and arrange cards in a circle.

   Give each group of students a set of life-cycle event flashcards. Ask them to put the events in order. Have students write a sentence describing what each event signifies and arrange cards in a line.

   Ask students to compare and contrast the two calendars of Jewish events *(one is annual, communal, and established; the other is personal and variable).*
3. (15 minutes) Have students read **To Everything There Is a Season** (page 6) as a class and do the activity **Jewish Times**. Which of King Solomon's times might relate to many of the Jewish times? *(dance, laugh, cry)* Why? *(We demonstrate many emotions at these events.)* Have students complete **Your Turn** on page 7. Share responses.
4. **Experiential Learning:** (15 minutes) Have students create a personal Jewish Times album by decorating and personalizing a file folder. Ask students to create a word picture or illustrations of some of the Jewish times they have experienced. Keep the folders in school, and have students add to their albums after holidays; after school, synagogue, and life-cycle events; and after certain upcoming lessons.

Wrapping It Up: (5 minutes) Have students share what they think is the best feature of Jewish holidays and life-cycle events.

The Tech Connection: Add to the classroom atmosphere by playing a video of the song "Turn, Turn, Turn" by Pete Seeger and the Byrds as students complete the activities related to the Ecclesiastes text. Several versions are available by searching for "turn turn turn" at www.youtube.com.

Building Jewish Identity • Teacher's Lesson Plan Manual

SACRED TIME

CHAPTER 1: LESSON 2

How do we make time into Jewish time?

Lesson Objectives: Students will be able to:
1. Explain the role of blessings in Jewish tradition.
2. Explain that saying the Sheheheyanu sanctifies time.
3. Cite times that are appropriate for recitation of the Sheheheyanu.

Getting Started: (5 minutes)
Ask students to suggest ways that we highlight something that we want people to notice, both in class and at home *(we hang it up on the bulletin board, we paint it a bright color, we enlarge it)*. Tell them that Jewish tradition provides a way for us to notice something of importance. We stop and say blessings as a way of taking notice of something that we value.

Exploring the Text:
1. (10 minutes) Read the Sheheheyanu blessing **(page 7)** and its translation. For what are we expressing our gratitude? *(time, life)* Ask students how the meaning of the Sheheheyanu differs from other blessings that they know *(other blessings are about foods or doing mitzvot)*. Why is there a blessing for our lives and for time? *(We often take things for granted.)*

2. (10 minutes) Have students do the exercise **Noting New Experiences** (page 7). Share responses. Point out that the Sheheheyanu expresses our gratitude and appreciation for the things we have and the experiences we enjoy. Typically there are times, such as festivals and most life-cycle events, when recitation of the Sheheheyanu is part of the ritual. However, we can find many other times of our lives when it is appropriate for us to be appreciative of an opportunity or an experience. Have students brainstorm a list of those times. Ask students to share some of their possible Sheheheyanu moments and add their list to their Jewish Times album.

3. **Experiential Learning:** (20 minutes) Divide students into small groups. Ask that they determine a moment in their lives that would be appropriate for the recitation of the Sheheheyanu. Have them act out the event, then share what recitation of the Sheheheyanu would have added to the time *(a sense of gratitude, importance, uniqueness)*.

Wrapping It Up: (5 minutes) Ask students to complete the following sentence: "The Sheheheyanu is like a … because it …" *(a flashlight because it illuminates something, cold water because it wakes you up)*.

The Tech Connection: Encourage students to make note of their Sheheheyanu moments throughout the school year on your Online Learning Center classroom space or the class blog.

SACRED TIME: THE JEWISH CALENDAR AND LIFE CYCLE
CHAPTER 2: Making Time for the Jewish Week — LESSON 1

What is a Jewish week?

Lesson Objectives: Students will be able to:
1. Explain why days begin at sunset on the Jewish calendar.
2. Cite differences between a Jewish and a secular week.
3. Name the days of the week in Hebrew and explain the numbers on the Hebrew clock.

Materials Needed: Copies of Genesis 1:1–5; pairs of index cards, each with the name of a Hebrew or English day of the week written on it

Getting Started: (5 minutes)
Ask students how they know a new day has begun *(the alarm rings, the sun rises)*. Tell students that they are going to be Jewish detectives and discover another way of determining when a new day begins.

Exploring the Text:
1. (5 minutes) Divide students into study partner groups. Distribute copies of Genesis 1:1–5. Based on the text, ask students to determine when the days begin on the Jewish calendar. What can this teach us about how Jews think about time? *(Jewish ideas about time involve Torah and tradition.)*
2. (10 minutes) Ask students to do the activity **Counting the Days and Making Them Count** (page 9). Practice the days of the week by repeating them in order as a class. Have students practice further in study partner groups by one partner reciting a day of the week and the other providing the next day.
3. (5 minutes) Ask students to do the activity **Hebrew Time** (page 9). Working in study partner groups and using the Hebrew letters as numbers, have students create simple addition problems for one another. Answers can exceed a total of 12 if responses are given in English but are limited to 12 if problems are answered in Hebrew.
4. **Experiential Learning:** (15 minutes) Give each student one card of a pair. Ask that students find one that has the translation of their day. Once all students have found a match, have them exchange cards with other students and find their new match. Repeat several times. Recite the Hebrew days of the week as a class, encouraging volunteers to try it as pairs or individuals. Have students share their week with one another, introducing their activities using the Hebrew day of the week (for example, "*B'yom rishon, ani* go to my grandmother's house").

Wrapping It Up: (5 minutes) Have students complete the phrase "A Jewish week is …," with each student repeating each previous statement and adding their own contribution.

The Tech Connection: Have students make Hebrew signs for each day of the week and other classroom vocabulary. If you do not have a Hebrew keyboard or word processing program, students can produce the signs using the Hebrew Sign Maker: www.my-hebrew-programs.com/hsm.

SACRED TIME

CHAPTER 2: LESSON 2

What can Shabbat add to our Jewish week?

Lesson Objectives: Students will be able to:

1. Explain that their days are filled with demands.
2. Cite Shabbat as a Jewish tradition designed to offer relief from the ordinary.
3. Plan ways of bringing Shabbat into their lives.

Materials Needed: Index cards with adjectives describing days (from pressured to peaceful), clock template

Getting Started: (5 minutes)

Ask students to associate adjectives on the index cards with days of the week (*long—Monday, testing day—Friday, exhausting—Wednesday*). Ask students which adjectives they wish they could have used to describe more of their days (*unhurried, peaceful, relaxing*).

Exploring the Text:

1. (5 minutes) Shabbat answers our need for a day out of regular time. As a class, read **A Shabbat State of Mind** and **Shabbat in the Torah** (page 10). The Torah teaches us why we make a day holy, set apart, and our customs teach us some ways we might do it.

2. (5 minutes) Read **Words to Know** on page 11. Ask students to think of other ways to make Shabbat different and connected to God. Ask students to read or act out their ideas. As students are sharing, list their ideas on the board.

3. (5 minutes) Read **Only the Best for Shabbat** (page 12) as a class. Ask students what they can contribute of their personal best to Shabbat (*bringing a good attitude, trying a new food or family activity*). Have students set the Shabbat table with their favorite Shabbat items in **All Set for Shabbat** (page 12), adding what they will personally contribute.

4. **Experiential Learning:** (15 minutes) Have each student complete their own Shabbat clock templates, including what they might be freed *from* on Shabbat and what they might be free *to* do on Shabbat. Encourage them to try one thing from each of their lists during this coming Shabbat.

Wrapping It Up: (5 minutes) Ask students to write one sentence about how they might make Shabbat special this week. Have students share their idea and place their sentence into their Jewish Times album.

The Tech Connection: Search Google for a variety of hallah recipes. Include recipes on your Online Learning Center classroom space or class blog. Encourage students to try one of the recipes in the coming weeks.

SACRED TIME: THE JEWISH CALENDAR AND LIFE CYCLE
CHAPTER 3: Celebrating the Jewish Year — LESSON 1

What is a Jewish year?

Lesson Objectives: Students will be able to:
1. Compare and contrast the Jewish (lunar-solar) year with the secular (solar) year.
2. Define and explain Rosh Ḥodesh.
3. Connect the idea of Rosh Ḥodesh with the idea of newness.

Materials Needed: Venn diagram blanks, Jewish calendar for the month of your lesson, writing paper

Getting Started: (5 minutes)

Ask students to brainstorm what makes up a year *(12 months, one school grade to another, 365 days, the pages on the calendar, expiration of a magazine subscription).* We have lots of ways to measure a year, and the Jewish people have a way that is unique. It involves celestial bodies and getting them to work together rather than colliding.

Exploring the Text:
1. (10 minutes) Students read **Good Night Moon** (page 15) in study partner groups, using the Venn diagram to compare and contrast the secular year with the Jewish year. Summarize the contrasts.
2. (5 minutes) Distribute a Jewish calendar for the current month. Find any Jewish holidays. When in the lunar cycle do they occur? When does Rosh Ḥodesh occur? What will the moon look like today? Is it growing smaller or larger at this time of the month? Is the moon "waxing" or "waning"?
3. (10 minutes) Read **Words to Know** (page 15), and ask students to create a "new month's resolution" for the new month in the class. Ask students to reflect and contribute ideas about what they can begin anew as a group *(being better friends, everyone participating in school services).*
4. **Experiential Learning:** (15 minutes) Divide students into study partner groups to create a personal "New Idea for a New Moon." The idea might be expressed using a poem, a slogan, or a dramatization. Have each study partner group share their idea in a "Rosh Ḥodesh Roundup."

Wrapping It Up: (5 minutes) Have students write a memo to themselves, indicating what they would like to begin in the coming month. Have them place these notes in their Jewish Times album.

The Tech Connection: Encourage students to send Rosh Ḥodesh greetings to the women in their lives using www.babaganewz.com/ecards/have-a-joyous-rosh-hodesh or to design their own Rosh Ḥodesh greeting cards using a personalized e-card creator tool, such as www.buzzle.com/cards-create.asp or www.someecards.com/usercards/create.

SACRED TIME

CHAPTER 3: LESSON 2

How do we make the year Jewish?

Lesson Objectives: Students will be able to:

1. Explain that Jews live in two months simultaneously—one Hebrew and one secular.
2. Share the date of their birthday on the Hebrew calendar.
3. Demonstrate a holiday skill that is new to them.

Materials Needed: One calendar page with no notations, one calendar page filled in with personal events, Hebrew/secular calendar page with Torah portions and candle-lighting times, blank Hebrew calendar with no secular dates for the remainder of the school year, perpetual calendar or computer with Internet access, supplies for the Calendar-Go-Round

Getting Started: (5 minutes)
Display the pair of calendar pages, and ask students how they differ (*one gives you no information; the other lists things the user believes to be important*). Distribute the Hebrew calendar page, and have students list what information they see on the page.

Exploring the Text:

1. (15 minutes) Look at the calendar **It's About Time** (page 17). What time does it show? (*Jewish and secular*) Whose times are they? (*Ours—Jews live in both times.*) Remind students that when they learned about the lunar year, they learned that lunar months are shorter than the months of the secular year. We learn to make the two calendars live together. Distribute the Hebrew calendars, and tell students the current Hebrew date. Have students complete the English dates for the remainder of the months. Have students place their completed months in their Jewish Times album. Begin future classes with a volunteer announcing the Hebrew calendar date.

    As students are working on Activity 1, ask each student in turn to tell you his or her birthdate (and if they know what time of day they were born), and help them look up their Hebrew birthdates. Have students whose birthdays occur during the remainder of the school year mark it on their calendars.

2. (5 minutes) Have students complete the exercises **It's About Time** (page 16) and **Giving It Your All for the Jewish Holidays** (pages 18–19).

3. **Experiential Learning:** (20 minutes) Create a Calendar-Go-Round, with stations around the classroom, allowing students to complete their choice of activities. This is an opportunity for students to acquire new celebratory skills. For example, stations might include activities such as rolling a beeswax Ḥanukkah candle, eating an Israeli fruit, selecting a favorite haggadah, putting together a *lulav* from paper components, practicing saying *Ḥag Sameaḥ*, folding paper *hamantashen* by forming a circle into a triangle, and so on.

Wrapping It Up: (5 minutes) Have students share a holiday skill at which they hope to become more proficient, then create a "Note to Self" for their Jewish Times album.

The Tech Connection: Create customized Jewish calendars for any year at www.hebcal.com/hebcal. Hebrew calendar conversion sites like this one, www.hebcal.com/converter, will enable you to find students' Hebrew birthdates.

SACRED TIME: THE JEWISH CALENDAR AND LIFE CYCLE
CHAPTER 4: The First Steps in a Jewish Life — LESSON 1

In what unique ways do we take our first Jewish steps?

Lesson Objectives: Students will be able to:
1. Cite the three categories into which blessings fall.
2. Explain the blessings we say upon the celebration of a new baby.
3. Explain the concept of "being part of the act" and share how they accomplished it.

Materials Needed: Copies of blessings that express gratitude, praise, and wishes; materials appropriate to your selection of the ceremonial art piece students will create

Getting Started: (5 minutes)
Explain that we say blessings for three main purposes: to articulate our thanks, to praise God, and to express our wishes. Distribute copies of blessings to small groups of students, and ask that they sort and categorize them. Ask for models of each type of blessing. Why might we say each type of blessing upon the birth or adoption of a new baby? (*We feel all of the emotions they express.*)

Exploring the Text:
1. (10 minutes) Ask students to read **A New Jewish Life** (page 20) silently, underlining the blessing that is said at a *brit milah*. What function do these blessings serve? (*They express our wishes.*) These wishes fall into three categories: Jewish connection, family, and actions. Ask each student to create a blessing that falls into each of the categories appropriate to the birth or adoption of a new baby. Share the blessings.

2. (10 minutes) Read **It's a Boy!** (page 21) aloud as a class. What is the intent of circumcision? (*It is a physical sign of the covenant between God and Abraham.*) Read **It's a Girl!** (page 21) aloud, asking that students underline the similarities between the events of the *brit milah* and *brit bat* ceremonies (*recitation of blessings and other texts, announcement of the baby's name, and the sharing of a festive meal*) as they read. The *s'udat mitzvah* is a meal that is held upon the performance of a mitzvah. Why do students think that we celebrate by eating? Have students create a list of responses in study partner groups (*for example, a celebration should be a lengthy event; it's a way for the hosts to give something to their guests*). Share responses.

3. **Experiential Learning:** (20 minutes) Have students read **A Welcome Tradition** and **Honoring Special Moments** (page 22), finding Tobi Kahn's rationale for creating ceremonial art for his family. Welcome students to become a "part of the act" by creating an art piece for their family (for example, a wall hanging, a table runner). The piece might commemorate their own birth ceremony, like the *wimpel* and chairs, including the Hebrew date of their birth or Jewish symbols.

Wrapping It Up: (5 minutes) Ask students to summarize the components of life-cycle events that are traditional and those in which we might make choices.

The Tech Connection: Students can draw their ceremonial art pieces online using free online whiteboard programs like www.scriblink.com, www.dabbleboard.com, or www.flockdraw.com. Share images of students' ceremonial art on your Online Learning Center classroom space or the class blog.

Building Jewish Identity • Teacher's Lesson Plan Manual

SACRED TIME
CHAPTER 4: LESSON 2

What paths are there in a Jewish life?

Lesson Objectives: Students will be able to:

1. Explain the Jewish tradition regarding names.
2. Make clear that there are varied paths in Jewish lives.
3. Express portions of their own Jewish paths.

Materials Needed: Paper, pencils, highlighters, copies of foot/shoe graphics

Getting Started: (10 minutes)

Ask students to think of the oldest relative they have. Ask them to write down all of that person's names (for example, Mr./Mrs., first name, Hebrew name, professional titles, honorary titles, nicknames, names family members call them). Have students circle the name(s) the person was given by his or her parents, underline the names other people call him or her, and highlight the names that the person earned him- or herself. What observations can students make about how we are named? *(We are given names in many ways.)*

Exploring the Text:

1. (15 minutes) Read the narrative **What's In a Name?** (page 24) as a class, and ask students to do the activity that follows. Our names also reflect who we are in different ways. Read the following text from Ecclesiastes Rabbah: "In life, you discover that people are called by three names: one is the name the person is called by his father and mother, one is the name people call him, and one is the name he acquires for himself. The best one is the one he acquires for himself." Ask: Why is the name we acquire for ourselves the best one? *(It gives us a goal; it really reflects who we are.)* What are some of the best names that students think a person might earn? *(caring, loving, good friend)* Have students create a piece of word art that includes several of their names, including their Hebrew name, and place it in their Jewish Times album.

2. (5 minutes) Read **More than One Path to a Jewish Life** (page 23). Explain that we can think of our Jewish lives as long paths or roads. Being born Jewish is one way to start down that path, but it is only the first step of a journey down the road. Have students sketch different types of roads or paths and describe their path to the class *(it's smooth and straight, it's bumpy, it is a toll road)*. Summarize that, like the students' roads, our paths differ, but each has crossed in the classroom.

3. **Experiential Learning:** (15 minutes) Ask students to depict their Jewish path by selecting a number of people or experiences that have influenced their Jewish lives and writing each on a paper outline of a foot or shoe. The people might be family members or others, even historic figures whose stories have impacted them. If possible, tape feet to the walls leading to your classroom door or post on a bulletin board.

Wrapping It Up: (5 minutes) Ask students to name their own Jewish path. Is it Long Winding Road? Is it Smooth Sailing Street or Rocky Road?

The Tech Connection: Make a word collage of all the names of students' oldest relatives using a word cloud generator like www.tagxedo.com or www.imagechef.com/ic/word_mosaic. For added fun, form the word cloud in the shape of a shoe, representing the person's individual path.

SACRED TIME: THE JEWISH CALENDAR AND LIFE CYCLE
CHAPTER 5: Preparing to Be a Jewish Adult — LESSON 1

How do we prepare to become a Jewish adult?

Lesson Objectives: Students will be able to:
1. Explain that becoming a Jewish adult involves a process of learning.
2. Teach a piece of Torah.
3. Display their ability to read the *alef bet* from the Torah.

Materials Needed: A list of *mitzvot* appropriate for students, perpetual calendar of Torah portions or computer with Internet access, age-appropriate Torah summaries or textbooks

Getting Started: (5 minutes) Ask students to list the steps necessary for someone to learn to ride a bike. Go through the same process for high school graduation. What steps are needed for someone to become a bar or bat mitzvah? Emphasize that the steps take place in different areas—learning/living (which begins at birth), and then there are bar mitzvah–specific steps (for example, selecting Torah honors, planning a party).

Exploring the Text:
1. (10 minutes) Read **Preparing for the Big Day** (page 30), emphasizing that all of students' Jewish life experiences prepare them to become a Jewish adult. Reinforce the fact that everyone has questions about what it means to become a bar or bat mitzvah. Have students write their questions, one per slip of paper. Have students exchange questions and respond to one another in small groups. The questions that seem most appropriate might be sent to post–bar or bat mitzvah students, asking for their responses.

2. (15 minutes) As students are doing Activity 1, have each student in turn look up the Torah portion of their birth week with your assistance and read selections from it. Have students prepare to teach one sentence of the *parashah* of their birth week to the class, then present their teachings in Torah portion order. Emphasize that they have already done one of the acts expected of a Jewish adult—learning and teaching Torah. Ask students to place their materials and their teaching in their Jewish Times album.

3. **Experiential Learning:** (15 minutes) One of the anticipated challenges of becoming a bar or bat mitzvah is reading Torah without vowels or punctuation. Give students an opportunity to try it by giving each student a copy of the Sh'ma or V'ahavta without vowels and in Torah script. Have students work in study partner groups to find as many letters of the *alef bet* as they can. Encourage students to find words they recognize.

Wrapping It Up: (5 minutes) Students offer adjectives describing how it felt to be able to read Hebrew as it appears in the Torah.

The Tech Connection: Encourage students to watch a video about the Torah portion of their birth week on www.g-dcast.com. G-dcast videos are short, animated films and are available for each *parashah*.

SACRED TIME

CHAPTER 5: LESSON 2

How can I prepare to be a Jewish adult?

Lesson Objectives: Students will be able to:
1. Explain that becoming a Jewish adult is a process of action.
2. Design mitzvah projects based on needs they identify within their own community.

Materials Needed: None

Getting Started: (5 minutes) Post the following question on the board: "What are you doing now to improve the world?" Instruct students to discuss their responses with a partner. Encourage students to think creatively about their answers. What do all the answers have in common? *(They require action.)*

Exploring the Text:
1. (5 minutes) Read **One Mitzvah Follows Another** (page 32), emphasizing that mitzvah projects and tzedakah projects are some ways that students can actively work to improve the world.

2. (5 minutes) Ask students why they think mitzvah projects are part of the bar or bat mitzvah preparations. What does this active participation in a mitzvah project have to do with the process of becoming a Jewish adult? Read **Pay It Forward** (page 32), and tell students that they will complete the chain of events shortly.

3. **Experiential Learning:** (25 minutes) Divide students into three groups—social action, environment, and spiritual realm. Take all the students on a community walk in which each group assesses the needs of the community in their assigned category. Upon returning to the classroom, students should use the observations they made on the walk to devise projects based on the needs they identified. For example, the environment group might notice that there is a lot of litter in the community. To address this concern, it could schedule a community cleanup to raise awareness. Have students complete the chain of events on **page 32** for the mitzvah project idea they identified on the community walk.

4. (5 minutes) Read **A Lifelong Commitment** (page 33), and ask students to brainstorm ways to continue their Jewish learning after their bar or bat mitzvah.

Wrapping It Up: (5 minutes) As a class, vote on which of the three mitzvah projects identified on the community walk to implement over the remainder of the school year. Ask: What makes our project uniquely Jewish even if it serves a segment of the population outside the Jewish community? How will actively working on this project help prepare us for Jewish adulthood?

The Tech Connection: Students can use an online tool like www.flowchart.com to easily create a visual representation of the sequence of events in the process of developing a mitzvah project.

SACRED TIME: THE JEWISH CALENDAR AND LIFE CYCLE
CHAPTER 6: Establishing a Jewish Home
LESSON 1

How do we begin to build a Jewish home?

Lesson Objectives: Students will be able to:
1. List the major events of a Jewish wedding ceremony and what values they demonstrate.
2. Explain the role of the Sheva B'rachot (Seven Blessings) of the wedding ceremony.
3. Use the Hebrew word for marriage, explain its meaning, and cite how it is displayed in the wedding ceremony.

Materials Needed: Shabbat candle, Ḥanukkah candle, matzah, highlighters, copies of the Sheva B'rachot (enlarged text for ease of use)

Getting Started: (5 minutes) Remind students that symbols tell a story of what we value. Ask students what each of the ritual items symbolize. What story does each tell about what we value? *(Creation, Jewish history, freedom)*

Exploring the Text:
1. (10 minutes) Remind students that Jewish rituals are built with symbols—even the Jewish wedding. Distribute highlighters. As a class, have students read from **Pages from a Jewish Wedding Album** (pages 34–35). As students read, ask that they highlight all the symbols they find in the wedding ceremony. Compile a list of all the symbols that students found. Assign each student a symbol, and ask that they write a sentence about the values they find represented in it *(wine—sharing; ring—reminder of one another)*. Have all students read the values they discovered.

2. (15 minutes) Read **Words to Know**: Sheva B'rachot (page 37). Distribute copies of the Sheva B'rachot. Have students work in study partner groups and mark the copy as indicated for each mention of the following in the blessings:
God—Star of David; joy—smiley face; history—arrow pointing left; future—arrow pointing right; bride and groom—circle around both; *Am Yisrael*/Eretz Yisrael—underline; all people—stick figure

3. **Experiential Learning:** (15 minutes) Divide students into small groups, assigning each group one of the *b'rachot*. Ask that the group members use their bodies to depict the meaning of their *b'rachah* (blessing). The group might choose to form a statue or represent the meaning through motion. They might be silent or use sound to add to their depiction.

Wrapping It Up: (5 minutes) The Hebrew word for marriage is *kiddushin*. Its root tells us that holiness is part of its meaning. Ask students where they find holiness in the wedding ceremony *(the sharing by the bride and groom, the memory of God and Jewish history)*.

The Tech Connection: Students can use www.thinglink.com to make their parents' wedding photos (or a Jewish wedding photo you provide) interactive, by adding tags or electronic markers to the images. For example, have students tag the *ḥatan*, the *kalah*, the *ḥupah*, and so on.

SACRED TIME
CHAPTER 6: LESSON 2

What makes a home Jewish?

Lesson Objectives: Students will be able to:
1. Characterize a Jewish home as a place in which people reflect Jewish values and beliefs.
2. Define *sh'lom bayit* as the value of creating peace in the home.
3. Explain the symbolism of the mezuzah in Jewish tradition.

Materials Needed: Blocks or building bricks, mezuzah-making supplies, (optional) parchment copies

Getting Started: (5 minutes) Ask a student volunteer to use the building bricks to create a simple house. Tell students that the same components can be used to build very different houses. Ask a second volunteer to build another, very different house with the building bricks. Explain that, like houses, no two families are exactly alike. Even if your house is the same design as all your neighbors', your family has made choices that make yours unique. The same is true of every family and every Jewish family.

Exploring the Text:
1. (5 minutes) How can we identify a Jewish home? Read **A Blessed House** (page 38) as a class. Every mezuzah tells the Jewish home story. What is that story? Ask students to contribute one phrase to a single oral story created by the entire class.

2. (10 minutes) The mezuzah reminds us that Jewish values are lived within the house and are carried when we leave. Read **Give a Little Respect** (page 39). *Sh'lom bayit*, peace in the house, is a Jewish value that requires every family member to contribute some ingredient to making it happen. Divide students into study partner groups, and ask that they create an ingredient list *(for example, patience, understanding)* to add to the class recipe for *sh'lom bayit*. Have students save their recipe in their Jewish Times albums.

3. **Experiential Learning:** (25 minutes) Ask students to do the activity **Design in Reach** (page 39), then actually create a mezuzah cover for the doors to their rooms using their design. Remind students that all *mezuzot* contain a parchment scroll and have the letter *shin*, representing God's name, on their cover. The decorative aspects of the mezuzah cover can reflect personal interests, favorite colors or images, and so on. Send home a note explaining that a handwritten mezuzah scroll should be placed inside the student-created covers.

Wrapping It Up: (5 minutes) What can a Jewish home be? Ask each student to complete the following sentence: "A Jewish home is …"

The Tech Connection: Take pictures of students' mezuzah cover creations, and share the images on www.flickr.com.

SACRED TIME: THE JEWISH CALENDAR AND LIFE CYCLE
CHAPTER 7: Mourning a Loss the Jewish Way — LESSON 1

How do Jewish traditions help ease the loss of a loved one?

Lesson Objectives: Students will be able to:
1. Articulate that mourning traditions are intended to honor the deceased and help the mourners.
2. Explain the tradition of reciting a blessing when visiting a mourner.
3. Cite the importance of following the lead of the mourners.

Materials Needed: None

Getting Started: (5 minutes)

Note: Before beginning this lesson, ask your education director if any students in your class have suffered a recent loss. If so, you might wish to communicate with a parent or guardian before the lesson.

Remind students that Jewish tradition accompanies us through the best times of our lives. Introduce this lesson by telling them that it also helps us support one another during the worst moments. Ask students to list how we normally support one another in a difficult time *(being a good listener, providing what people need)*.

Exploring the Text:
1. (5 minutes) Have students read **Giving It Time** (page 40) as a class. Brainstorm the needs of a mourner and list suggestions on the board *(time to talk, time to be silent, food, important errands done)*. Divide students into study partner groups, and ask that they create roles for community members based on the list they created. What are specific roles that students can play? *("being there" for friends, caring for the yard or pets at the house of mourning)*

2. (5 minutes) Read **Giving Comfort** (page 41) as a class. What does the blessing say? What doesn't it say? For whom is this blessing intended, and how does it help them? *(Mourners—it helps them to acknowledge their loss, not feel alone.)*

3. (10 minutes) Read **The First Days** and **The Week After** (pages 40–41) as a class, with students underlining the traditions that support mourners and circling those that honor the departed. Have students continue reading silently until the end of page 41, underlining and circling the practices mentioned.

4. **Experiential Learning:** (20 minutes) It is a mitzvah to pay a *shiva* visit. We perform this mitzvah out of caring, but we are often uncertain of what to do. Have students meet in small groups to generate a list of their questions regarding paying a *shiva* visit. Have groups share their questions and suggest responses. Create a list of responses to the most frequently asked questions.

Wrapping It Up: (5 minutes) Have students summarize the ways we can support someone in mourning *(talking/being silent, crying/smiling)*. Be certain to emphasize that there are no incorrect answers when we follow the lead of the mourners.

The Tech Connection: Students can create a timeline of the mourning process using an online timeline tool, such as www.timetoast.com or www.xtimeline.com. Use fictitious dates if necessary.

SACRED TIME
CHAPTER 7: LESSON 2

How do Jewish mourning traditions help us to honor the departed?

Lesson Objectives: Students will be able to:
1. Explain that mourning traditions are intended to honor the departed.
2. Explain why we share communal mourning rituals.
3. List ways and places that their community remembers the departed.

Materials Needed: Photos of the Lincoln Memorial or another memorial, a tzedakah box, memorial plaque, *yahrtzeit* candle, pebble

Getting Started: (5 minutes) Divide students into study partner groups. Display the pictures. Allow students one minute to determine what the people and items depicted have in common *(they each depict a way of keeping someone's memory alive)*.

Exploring the Text:
1. (10 minutes) Read **Keeping Memories Alive** (page 42) as a class. Have students share information about the person after whom they are named and other ways their family remembers those who have passed away.

2. (5 minutes) Read **The Whole Community Remembers** and **Mourning the Temple** (page 43). Announce the dates of Yom Hashoah and Tisha B'Av, and have students mark Yom Hashoah on the calendars in their Jewish Times album. Why would we have customs that enable us to mourn people we never knew? *(to keep Jewish history, and the people, alive; teaching the community)*

3. (10 minutes) Ask students if there is someone whose memory they would like to remember. Have the class come to consensus on a person to honor. What was important to that person? Have students brainstorm ways to collect tzedakah to honor the person *(planting a tree, dedicating a library book)*.

4. **Experiential Learning:** (15 minutes) Students will design a tzedakah project to raise funds for the purpose designated in Activity 3. Students should volunteer for one of the necessary working groups: fund-raising ideas, written publicity, visual publicity, audio publicity, communication with recipient of collection, calendar of events. In each group a student should take notes of decisions made and further steps needed.

Wrapping It Up: (5 minutes) Ask students to share why they think it is important to memorialize the departed with concrete actions.

The Tech Connection: Students can choose a victim of the Holocaust to remember. Visit http://rememberme.ushmm.org/gallery for a list of names, along with photos and other information about each person.

SACRED TIME: THE JEWISH CALENDAR AND LIFE CYCLE
CHAPTER 8: This Jewish Life — LESSON 1

What defines a Jewish life?

Lesson Objectives: Students will be able to:
1. Explain that a Jewish life is defined by times that are fixed.
2. Cite ways that fixed times can become personal statements of tradition.
3. Share their ideas about making Jewish times their own.

Materials Needed: Small sticky notes

Getting Started: (5 minutes) Have students cite ways that we share the same times in a variety of ways *(sports we play, books we choose)*. Ask students to name some Jewish times that we share with one another *(holidays, life-cycle events)*.

Exploring the Text:
1. (10 minutes) Have students play the game on **pages 44–45**.
2. (15 minutes) Ask students to write two additional game spaces for each game section (Getting Started, Growing Up, Bar/Bat Mitzvah Time, Becoming an Adult, Adult Life), thinking about the following: How can they adapt the game board to make it more personal? What choices might they make? How might they bring their own style and interests to some observance? Have students write their game space ideas on individual sticky notes labeled with the appropriate game section.
3. **Experiential Learning:** (15 minutes) Have students create a game board on a bulletin board, using their sticky notes as game spaces. Arrange the game spaces according to game section (Getting Started, Growing Up, Bar/Bat Mitzvah Time, Becoming an Adult, Adult Life). For each game section, summarize the posted ideas. Which ideas do students find interesting? Might they adopt the idea or adapt it?

Wrapping It Up: (5 minutes) Have students explain the importance of having fixed observances, while having the opportunity to personalize them *(making something our own makes us feel comfortable, creative, or powerful)*.

The Tech Connection: Summarize student learning by creating a game of Jeopardy unique to the class knowledge base at http://jeopardylabs.com.

SACRED TIME — CHAPTER 8: LESSON 2

What is unique about your Jewish life?

Lesson Objectives: Students will be able to:

1. Cite some of their recent Jewish learning.
2. Relate experiences in which they have participated.
3. Describe their Jewish goals.

Materials Needed: Several books on the same subject (such as biographies of the same person, cookbooks, sports-related books), blank books, art materials, snack

Getting Started: (5 minutes) Display a few books on the same subject. What do they have in common? How do they differ? Why do they differ? *(Each author tells the story in his or her own way or conveys information that each feels is important.)* How is being Jewish similar? *(We each tell our Jewish stories differently.)* Tell students that this lesson will give them an opportunity to tell their own Jewish story.

Exploring the Text:

1. (5 minutes) Read **Staying Centered** (page 46), and have students complete the Magen David activity.
2. (5 minutes) Distribute blank books and set out art materials for students to create original books to tell their own Jewish stories. Ask students to think about the items they included on their Magen David, about the information they learned about the Jewish calendar and life cycle, and about their Jewish lives. Students should then come up with a title that expresses something unique about their own Jewish experiences and goals.
3. (5 minutes) Have students plan out a table of contents, including what they will include on each page of their book. Distribute students' Jewish Times albums for reference. Brainstorm or offer possibilities for page topics, including the following: I have learned … , I follow traditions … , Ways I am creative … , I look forward … , I have thought about … , I can contribute … , I try to … , I have succeeded at … , Something I want to learn more about … , Something I want to try … , Using all my senses Jewishly …
4. (15 minutes) Invite students to create their pages in any way they choose (illustration, word art, poetry, collage, abstract art, sentences).

Wrapping It Up: (15 minutes) Host a *siyum* (the traditional celebration that takes place at the conclusion of a course of Jewish learning) to celebrate the students' conclusion of this aspect of their learning. Have each student present one page of their Jewish Times album or the book of their Jewish story. Enjoy a celebratory snack, too!

The Tech Connection: Students can create a digital version of their books using Bookr, www.pimpampum.net/bookr, an online Web book creation tool.

BUILDING JEWISH IDENTITY

PART 3
Activities for Jewish Holidays

INTRODUCTION

The building blocks of Jewish identity are intimately woven into every holiday observance and commemoration. Each Jewish holiday combines examples of our ethical heritage, myths and laws, symbols and rituals, Hebrew language, and artistic expressions. As a result, each annual holiday cycle provides the opportunity for identity building.

Making personal meaning creates identity. The classroom holiday experience can connect students to our past and enable them to make it meaningful in their lives.

Finding a place on the Jewish spectrum creates identity. Every Jewish holiday has the potential to build relationships within the congregation, the community, and the family. Classroom diversity introduces students to the variety of opinions, experiences, and heritage that compose the contemporary Jewish community.

Feeling proficient creates identity. With each holiday observance, students can grow in competence and comfort with our traditions and rituals. Classroom learning and experiences further develop skills and comfort.

In this section, you will find activities for teaching the Jewish holidays through the lens of building Jewish identity and many of the concepts introduced in the textbooks.

JEWISH HOLIDAYS — ACTIVITIES 1–2

ACTIVITY 1: High Holidays (Rosh Hashanah and Yom Kippur)

Symbols tell us stories of our past and invite us to tell our own stories. Here is a suggestion for looking at the shofar—one of the primary symbols of the High Holidays—and the role it might play in our own lives.

Divide students into five groups, giving each group one of the following texts:

- Group 1: Joshua 6:2–5
- Group 2: Exodus 19:16
- Group 3: Leviticus 23:23–24
- Group 4: Psalm 81:4
- Group 5: Psalm 150

Have students determine the role of the shofar in each text *(a call to battle, a symbol of God's presence, a reminder of the New Moon and holidays, a musical instrument)*. Each group creates a visual representation of the role of the shofar in their text.

Ask: What is the role of the shofar in our High Holiday services? Maimonides said that the call of the shofar is intended to wake us up and remind us to return to what we know God expects of us. Was Maimonides thinking of the shofar as an alarm clock, waking people who were actually asleep? Are there ways of being physically awake, yet "asleep"? What does it mean to be "asleep" when we use the word this way?

Play a recording of the shofar calls, or blow the shofar yourself. As students listen, ask them to think about "waking up" to some of their behaviors or to something around them. What might they do about it in the next year? Have students write themselves a "wake-up call."

ACTIVITY 2: Sukkot

- As a class, examine a real set of the four species. Tell students that the midrash compares the four species to parts of the body based on their shapes. The *lulav* is the spine, the *hadas* branches are the eyes, the *aravot* are the mouth, and the *etrog* is the heart. Have students take a closer look to understand how each species looks like the body part it symbolizes.

- On the line drawings of the four species (available at www.behrmanhouse.com/building-jewish-identity), have students write how they use their corresponding body part to do mitzvot. Why does being a Jew require a strong spine? What do we see when we look around? How can we use our mouths and hearts in Jewish ways?

JEWISH HOLIDAYS

ACTIVITY 3: Simḥat Torah

We rejoice in the gift of Torah and make the scroll the centerpiece of our Simḥat Torah celebration. We show our acceptance of Torah by the way we live our lives. Here are some ways to enable students to find and highlight the impact of Torah in our midst:

- Give students a supply of sticky notes, and have them walk around the class, school, and/or synagogue marking the "evidence" of Torah learning. Food collections, *mezuzot*, information about Israel, and tzedakah boxes are all evidence of how we live Torah. Don't forget to have them search synagogue newsletters and flyers as well.

- Have students brainstorm ways that we show that the Torah scroll is honored by the community *(the Torah's garments and placement, our standing when it is lifted and saying blessings of gratitude, the tradition of not turning one's back to the scroll when it is carried, honoring people by asking them to come to the Torah).* Go through a model Torah service and allow students to point out other ways they see that we show our respect for and love of Torah.

- Have students cite examples of Torah in their lives. Each student might contribute a page to a book about Torah that is presented to younger students.

ACTIVITY 4: Ḥanukkah

Ḥanukkah is a time to recognize miracles both "in those days" and "in this time." Ask your students to brainstorm a list of everyday miracles. Write the list on a long sheet of mural paper. If you are successful, this list should be very, very long. It should include a wide range of miracles in nature, in our bodies, in our ability to learn and think, national miracles, specific events, and even personal miracles. Assign a committee of students to add graphics to the list.

When the banner is finished, post it in the hallway of the school. (The modern Hebrew word for miracle is *nes*, which literally means "banner.") Attach a felt-tipped pen and invite passersby to continue to add to the list and publicize miracles. Give the "mural" an appropriate header, such as a quote from a Ḥanukkah blessing or the dreidel.

JEWISH HOLIDAYS — ACTIVITY 5

ACTIVITY 5: Tu BiShevat

Divide the class into two groups. Give one group a copy of Genesis 1:28 and the other group a copy of Psalm 24:1.

- *Genesis 1:28: "God blessed them and said to them, 'Be fruitful and multiply, fill the earth and master it; and rule over the fish of the sea, the birds of the sky, and all the living things that creep on earth.'"*
- *Psalm 24:1: "The earth is God's and all that it holds, the world and all its inhabitants."*

Ask each group to create a project to explain their assigned text. Each group should create a song, poem, poster, banner, or bumper sticker. Encourage students to participate in the activity that best suits their skills and interests.

After each group's presentation, have students form study partner groups with a student from the other group. Discuss: Does the world all belong only to God? If so, why did God give it to people to master? And what does it mean to master something? How can the two texts possibly work together? Students should combine their two texts into a one-sentence summary to help us understand what it means to be a guardian of the earth.

As a class, discuss: How can your new understandings lead to action in the coming school year? What can class members do in school to show that they are guardians of the earth? What actions can each student take in their homes and personal lives to demonstrate their understanding in concrete ways? Create a list of suggestions and intentions, and have students record how they acted on their learning to become guardians of the earth as the year goes on. Students might also share suggestions of earth-friendly items they have seen and read about.

JEWISH HOLIDAYS

ACTIVITY 6: Purim

After hearing the *Megillah* and before the traditional Purim carnival, extend Purim knowledge with some of the following activities:

- Ask students to play the roles of the major actors in the *Megillah*. Have other students interview them in talk-show format about their motivations, fears, and so on. Allow characters to speak to one another as well.

- Put Esther on trial for her actions in the *Megillah*. Is she guilty of hiding her Jewish identity just to become queen? Or did she pretend to be a non-Jew so that she could be in a position of power when it was needed?

- Indict Haman for crimes against the Jews. Of what crimes is he guilty? Have students use the *Megillah* text to prepare the charges against him. Or, indict Aḥashverosh for his role in the plot against the Jews. Of what crimes is he guilty? Have students use the *Megillah* text to prepare the charges against him.

- Create an award for Mordecai. For what should he be honored? Be certain that the award is named, and remember to have fun with it because it's Purim!

- Find God in the Purim story. Point out that God is not mentioned by any name but that one can find God in numerous places. For example, have students dramatize a simple version of the *Megillah*, allowing a panel of students to stop the action whenever they find God's presence.

- Spark a lively class discussion with the following questions: What can we learn from Aḥashverosh about listening to other people? How do we know who to listen to? What would you have said to Haman when he was hatching his plot against the Jews to change his mind? What can we learn from Esther about judging people without knowing all about them?

ACTIVITY 7: Passover

Here are some creative ways to engage students in preparation for the celebration of Passover:

- Create a class scrapbook of redemption stories, including the redemption from Egyptian slavery. Other redemption stories can be historical or personal. Brainstorm ideas as a class (*for example, family immigration stories, Operation Solomon*). Each student should be responsible for one page, including creating the text and illustrations for that page. Once the pages are complete, compile them into one book and make copies for each student to bring home and share during their Passover seders.

- Ask students to choose a Passover symbol or Jewish ritual item that is meaningful to them. Have students use that symbol or object to trigger personal writing, describing the symbol or object and why it's particularly meaningful to them.

- Have students create a blog for a personality from the Passover story, following the personality through important life events. Instruct students to customize the "Web page" to reflect what they think the tastes of the characters would be. For example: What color would Moses choose as his background? What pictures would Aaron post on his site? What tagline would Naḥshon ben Aminadav, who was first to step into the sea before it split, use for his heading? What would they list as their favorite Web sites?

JEWISH HOLIDAYS — ACTIVITIES 8–9

ACTIVITY 8: Yom Ha'atzma'ut

We traditionally celebrate birthdays with gifts and good wishes. Here are some ways to celebrate Israel with your students:

- Throw a birthday party for Israel. Have students decorate the classroom with pictures, posters, and maps of Israel. Have students sing "Yom Huledet Sameaḥ" or other birthday songs, and eat cake decorated with white and blue icing to look like the Israeli flag! (Don't forget to recite the correct *b'rachah* before eating.) Also serve imported Israeli snacks and play lively Hebrew music to add to the festive atmosphere.

- Learn to sing "Hatikvah," Israel's national anthem. You might have students sing along with a recording or a video on YouTube.

- Learn just a little more about some area of interest pertaining to Israel. Have students brainstorm questions and then search for answers online. For example: Where can you ski? What is the time and temperature? Who in the class has Israeli relatives? Where do they live?

- Take a "walking tour" of major cities by handing out street maps (available online) and giving students a starting point and a destination. How would they get from point A to point B? What did they pass on their route? Alternatively, try out Google's Street View of Israel.

- Laminate maps of Israel, and cut them up into puzzles of varying difficulty. See who can put the most pieces together in the shortest amount of time. Count the passing seconds in Hebrew.

ACTIVITY 9: Shavuot

Shavuot has a dual identity as an agricultural and historical observance. Celebrate both of Shavuot's identities with some of these suggestions:

- Count the days of the omer between Passover and Shavuot, and have students imagine what it was like between the Exodus from Egypt and the giving of the law at Sinai. Take a few minutes at the start of each class to have students act out imaginary scenarios.

- The holiday of Shavuot is related to the wheat harvest. Have students collect boxes of wheat cereals for donation to a local food bank where they will be distributed to children whose breakfast program ends with the end of the school year.

- Conduct a mock Jewish wedding to teach both about Jewish weddings and about the marriage of the Jewish people to God upon receiving the Torah at Sinai.

- Have students design and craft thank-you cards to show appreciation to those who have connected them to Sinai, including the rabbi, former teachers, parents, and so on.

- If your school conducts a confirmation ceremony on Shavuot, make a point of attending as a class and sending congratulatory cards to the students in the confirmation class. Have students interview the confirmation students about why they chose to continue their formal Jewish education after bar or bat mitzvah and what they have gained in the process.

BUILDING JEWISH IDENTITY

PART 4
Family Education Programs

INTRODUCTION

Jewish learning and identity development are not laboratory sciences. The information that students learn in class and the experiences that they have in the classroom are preparation for living a Jewish life. The school teaches literacy; the family provides the context.

Because Shabbat does not occur during class time, we need families to be our partners. Because parents are sometimes uncertain about their own Jewish learning and choices, they need our help. Together the school and the family can form an effective partnership with the mutual goal of developing students' Jewish identities.

KEEP IN MIND

- Parents choose to be part of the congregation and school. They share precious possessions with the congregation: their children, their time, and their money.

- Today's families are complicated and diverse. Before planning family education programs, learn about the reality of your students' families. As a result, you might find it appropriate to refer to parents generically as adults and to adult-student pairs as partners. We can be certain of their adulthood, but we don't always know their relationship to our students. The fact that they come to support a student in their Jewish exploration is all we need to know.

- There's room for everyone in Jewish life and Jewish family education. The parent who "doesn't know" might be the one who bakes, works with wood, plays an instrument, or throws clay. Find a place for a parent and they gain a sense of competence and community. Their children see a Jewish role model in their own home. And you have a staff of specialists to bring new experiences to your classroom.

- No one wants to establish what they don't know in public, especially in front of their children. If you ask for information, don't expect a parent to provide it. Instead, you can provide the content or the scenario and ask the family to make choices within the content.

- Cultivate commitment by scheduling with the family in mind. Give parents plenty of notice about a family event. Avoid planning events for the first day back from a vacation or at a time when working parents cannot attend. Prepare alternative options for families who cannot attend a particular event but still want to accomplish the goal of a scheduled program.

- Build family education events around the interests and skills of your students. Parents will usually support any endeavor that their children enjoy.

TECHNIQUES TO USE WITH FAMILIES

- **Text Study:** Text study is the perfect format for family learning. A parent need not have attended religious school to read a suitable text and offer an opinion. Using texts can level the playing field; whether a parent has previously studied the text or not, he or she has never had the family conversation in which you will engage them. For example, learn about the Maccabees and discuss if you would have joined them in the fight. Read a verse from the Torah and share a personal understanding.

- **Debate:** Disagreement is not our enemy; apathy is. When appropriate, ask for a family consensus and watch the action as parent and child debate a Jewish subject. For example: Did Abraham pass or fail that test by taking his son to the mountaintop? If you were Joseph, would you have given food to the brothers who sold you? If the Torah teaches that you have to pay your worker on the day he or she earned the wages, is it okay to tell the babysitter you'll pay him or her next week?

- **Diverse Viewpoints:** Use techniques that convey positive messages about diverse viewpoints. For example, ask a question and offer three or four possible responses. Assign a corner of the room to each response. Ask participants which response best represents their own viewpoint, and have them stand in the appropriate part of the room. Alternatively, you can use a long rope and clothespins to demonstrate that Jewish identity covers a vast number of options. Ask a question, and have participants place themselves on the continuum of viewpoints.

- **Discussion Guides:** Provide family discussion guides. This technique is suitable for any aspect of the curriculum. Supply a quote, text, or article, and ask families to talk about how they feel about it. Do they agree or disagree? What would they have done in similar circumstances? What prediction can they make about future events?

- **Parent Involvement:** Build family education events around the interests and skills of your parents. Adapt their skills to growing the Jewish life skills of your students. Perhaps the parent who is a chef will agree to teach latke making; the potter parent might agree to fire class menorahs; the parent who is a lawyer might talk about pro bono work for a local charity; or the graphic designer could help students create fabulous holiday greeting cards for a class tzedakah project. Parents will often happily agree to perform a function at which they feel skilled and that is not an open-ended commitment.

- **Build Friendships:** Do things together as a group of class families to strengthen the curriculum and the class community. Remind parents that students will look forward to religious school and are more apt to continue their Jewish education after bar or bat mitzvah if they have friends in the class. We also know that families are most likely to continue their relationship with the congregation when they find meaningful connections to it. Group activities might include visiting a local museum, conducting an event for a local senior residence, or collecting and donating toys for a worthy cause. Have a group *havdalah* ceremony followed by moon watching and pizza, or a movie night with falafel.

- **Build Community:** Help families live in community. Ask a parent to assume responsibility for sharing class family news so that everyone is "in the know." If a class family is struggling with illness or loss or celebrating the birth of a new baby, ask other class families to prepare meals or run errands for them. This will go a long way toward fostering a sense of community and belonging.
- **Book Group:** Have all families read the same (short) book and come together for a book discussion with bagels after school.
- **Class Family Exhibit:** Ask families to bring in a Jewish item that is special to them and to share with the class what makes it special. Be clear that these need not be heirlooms. Expand the event to include an opportunity to craft a new future heirloom, such as a mezuzah cover, under the guidance of class parents with applicable expertise.
- **Tzedakah Fair:** Lead families in organizing an informational tzedakah fair or fund-raising event in support of tzedakah organizations identified by the congregation or class.
- **Share Their Work:** Encourage parents to drop off and pick up their children at the classroom door so that students can show parents their work. A parent's question or comment is a spontaneous family education activity.
- **Dig Deeper:** Provide parents with Internet resources for further learning. Ask them to share sites of interest with other parents, too, using the class blog. In addition, make synagogue library books available at family education events and offer articles for the taking.
- **Celebrate Together:** Encourage families to share a group holiday celebration—perhaps one night of Hanukkah, bringing all of their lights and traditions together. Or, encourage families to become a sukkah-building brigade, helping each other build *sukkot* at their homes and following up by eating in each one. If your students have a service attendance requirement, consider inviting families to share a group Shabbat dinner or lunch as part of the experience.

BUILDING JEWISH IDENTITY

Assessments

Evaluation of student understanding and learning is a vital part of the teaching process. It is an ongoing process that enables you to determine the effectiveness of each lesson and the impact of the learning activities, making adjustments according to your observations. It also enables you to appreciate the individual learning profile of every student. Following are some suggestions for ongoing assessments:

1. Create a Jewish community bulletin board on which students post items of Jewish interest they find within the community. Have students add a few words to each item, indicating why they think it is of interest to class members. How does it relate to their learning?

2. Periodically ask students to share accounts of events in the synagogue and Jewish community in which they have participated. What role did they play? How did it make them feel? Would they play the same role again or try a different one?

3. Ask students to talk about Jewish life-cycle events they have attended in their families. Encourage class members to compare and contrast other students' memories with some of their own.

4. Have students write and perform a skit that demonstrates their understanding of the traditions of a Jewish holiday or life-cycle event. Students may pretend they are a family celebrating together and include a variety of traditions, rituals, and ritual objects as well as blessings, if possible.

5. Have students create posters that demonstrate what they have learned about a topic, including key vocabulary from the chapter as well as pictures and other important elements.

6. Add Hebrew words to the life of the classroom and encourage their use. Label classroom features and items, and use Hebrew nouns and phrases from the books, where appropriate. Post the phrases as you introduce them for students' reference. Students can add a check mark to the phrase sign once they have mastered it.

7. Institute an "I see my world through Jewish eyes" time for students to share observations and ideas. Ask students to share their "wow" moments when they realize they are wearing new lenses and seeing things in a new, and Jewish, way.

8. Keep anecdotal records throughout the year of students' participation in class discussions, making note of how eager they are to participate and how well they work in a group. Also note how often students raise their hands to answer content questions.

9. Ask students to keep a journal throughout the year in which they write and draw pictures associated with the lessons they are learning.

BUILDING JEWISH IDENTITY

Notes

www.ingramcontent.com/pod-product-compliance
Lightning Source LLC
Chambersburg PA
CBHW081220230426
43666CB00015B/2820